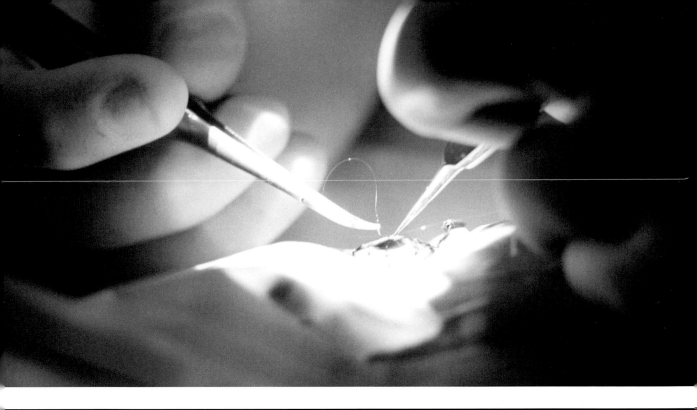

CUTTING EDGE MEDICINE

Organ Transplants

Carol Ballard

WORLD ALMANAC® LIBRARY

Please visit our Web site at: **www.garethstevens.com**
For a free color catalog describing World Almanac® Library's list of high-quality books
and multimedia programs, call 1-800-848-2928 (USA) or 1-800-387-3178 (Canada).
World Almanac® Library's fax: (414) 332-3567.

Library of Congress Cataloging-in-Publication Data available upon request from publisher.
Fax (414) 336-0157 for the attention of the Publishing Records Department.

Ballard, Carol.
      Organ transplants / Carol Ballard.
          p. cm. — (Cutting edge medicine)
      Includes bibliographical references and index.
      ISBN 978-0-8368-7868-4 (lib. bdg.)
      1. Transplantation of organs, tissues, etc.—Juvenile literature.   I. Title.
      RD120.76.B35   2007
      617.9'54—dc22   2006030902

This North American edition first published in 2007 by
World Almanac® Library
A Member of the WRC Media Family of Companies
330 West Olive Street, Suite 100
Milwaukee, WI 53212 USA

This U.S. edition copyright © 2007 by World Almanac® Library.
Original edition copyright © 2007 by Arcturus Publishing Limited.

Produced by Arcturus Publishing Limited.
Editor: Alex Woolf
Designer: Nick Phipps
Consultant: Dr. Eleanor Clarke

World Almanac® Library editor: Carol Ryback
World Almanac® Library designer: Kami M. Strunsee
World Almanac® Library art direction: Tammy West
World Almanac® Library production: Jessica Yanke and Robert Kraus

The right of Andrew Solway to be identified as the author of this work has been
asserted by him in accordance with the Copyright, Designs and Patents Act, 1988.

Photo credits: Getty Images: / 10. Rex: / TXM 16; / Action Press 22; / Mr. JCY 37. Science Photo Library: / J. L. Martra
/Publiphoto Diffusion 5, 38 ; / Mike Devlin 6; / Deep Light Productions 8, 12; / Kevin Beebe/Custom Medical Stock Photo 15;
/ Mauro Fermariello 19, 30; / National Cancer Institute 21; / Ed Young) 25; / Will and Deni McIntyre 26; / BSIP/Vem 29;
/ Michelle del Guercio 32; / Antonia Reeve 35; / BSIP/Platriez 40; / Maximillian Stock Ltd. 43; / A.J. Photo/Hop Americain 44;
/ Science Source 46; / Klaus Guldbrandsen 48; / Dr. Rob Stepney 51; / Peter Menzel 53; / Dr. Gary Gaugler 55; / Dr. Klaus
Boller 57; / Steve Gschmeissner 58.

Printed in China

1 2 3 4 5 6 7 8 9 10 10 09 08 07 06

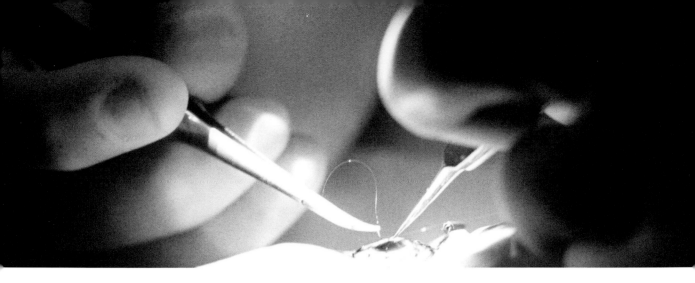

Contents

CHAPTER 1

What Is an Organ Transplant?

Most people are lucky enough to never worry about whether or not their body is working properly. They give no thought to how steady their heart is beating or if their kidneys are functioning. Other people, whose internal organs have become weakened by illness or disease, are not so lucky. These people must take a variety of medications every day just to stay alive or must spend hours every week hooked up to a machine that cleanses their blood. Sometimes, a severely damaged body organ cannot be fixed with medications or therapies. Then, the only option is to obtain a replacement organ. For example, when a healthy heart replaces a failing heart, normal blood circulation is restored. That person regains his or her health because of a heart transplant.

The heart is not the only organ that can be transplanted. Other body organs, such as skin and kidneys can be transplanted, too.

CUTTING EDGE SCIENCE

Body organization
Like all living things, the human body is made up of millions of tiny units called cells. Cells that have a similar structure and function are grouped together to make tissues. Tissues are grouped together to make organs, which are collections of tissues that perform a specific function. Organs that carry out similar or connected functions are grouped together to make systems. For example, lots of muscle cells make up muscle tissue. Muscle tissue, together with other connective tissues, make up the organ called the heart. The heart and other organs, such as blood vessels, make up the circulatory system.

Organ transplant operations are complex surgical procedures, requiring large medical teams—oftentimes in separate hospitals—as well as sophisticated medical equipment.

When is an organ transplant necessary?

An organ transplant may be needed for several reasons, including:

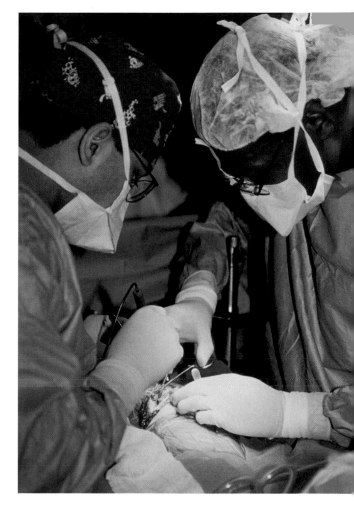

- a baby born with an organ or organs that are undeveloped or not properly developed, and the defects are inoperable;
- an organ irreversibly damaged by disease, age, or a hereditary condition that cannot be treated by medicines or other surgery;
- an organ damaged because of an accident and the injury is too serious or extensive to be repaired by another means.

A transplant is not always a suitable solution for a patient with a failing organ. In most cases, a transplant candidate must still be physically capable of withstanding the stress of undergoing general anesthesia, as well as the surgery itself. A lengthy recovery period often follows and may involve a strict regime of strong medications taken for life. Any patient who is too frail and weak from age or illness seldom receives a major organ transplant.

These surgeons are carrying out a liver transplant operation. A liver transplant is necessary if a patient is suffering severe liver disease and liver failure.

Types of organ transplant

There are four main types of organ transplant. Each is known as a "graft," which means joining together. The four types of transplant are called autograft, syngeneic graft, homograft, and xenograft.

Autograft is a transplant using a patient's own tissue. *Autograft* comes from the Greek word *autos*, which means "self." Another name for this type of transplant is "isograft," from the Greek word *isos*, meaning "equal."

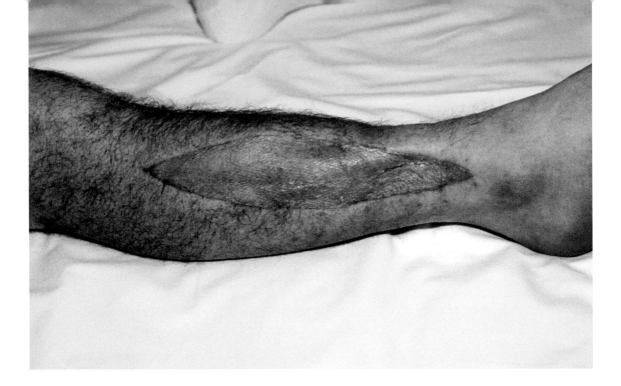

Autografts often play a major part in the treatment of patients with serious skin damage, for example, after a burn or some forms of surgery. If an area of skin is so badly damaged that it cannot repair itself, a skin graft may be removed from another part of the patient's body to repair the damaged area. Skin is among the body organs capable of repairing itself, and the area from which the tissue graft is taken will soon heal naturally.

The slightly darker elliptical patch on this man's leg is a skin graft that is healing well.

Syngeneic graft is an organ transplant from a genetically identical individual. A syngeneic graft can only occur during the transplant of an organ from one identical twin to the other—no other people have identical genes. "Syngeneic" comes from the Greek word *syngeneia*, which means "kinship."

Homograft is a transplant using an organ from an unrelated person. Many of the transplants that we hear most about, such as heart transplants, kidney transplants, and blood transfusions, are homografts. "Homograft" comes from the Greek word *homos*, which means "same" (that is, from the same species). Another name for this type of transplant is "allograft," from the Greek word *allos*, meaning "the other of two."

Xenograft is a transplant using an organ from two different species, such as a cow or a pig. An example of a xenograft is transplanting a heart valve from a cow or pig into a human, which is a common treatment for some types of heart valve problems. "Xenograft" comes from the Greek word *xenos*, meaning "foreign." Another name for this type of transplant is heterograft, from the Greek word *heteros,* meaning "the other of many."

Early history

The history of transplanting organs goes back thousands of years. Little evidence exists, however, to suggest that—except for some autografts, such as skin (*see page 8*)—any of the early attempts were successful. An organ transplant is a complicated procedure that involves a coordinated effort of assessing a recipient's condition, finding a suitable organ donor, arranging and performing the surgery, and establishing the follow-up care. Not until the twentieth century, when there were major advances in all branches of science and medicine, were organ transplants at a point where they could be successful or even routine procedures.

CUTTING EDGE   MOMENTS

Transplant milestones
Scientists have made a lot of progress since the early attempts at organ transplantation. This table shows just some of the many historic achievements in this branch of medicine.

year	place	organs transplanted
1906	Olmutz, Moravia (Czech Republic)	cornea (clear layer at front of eye)
1954	Boston, Massachusetts	kidney
1956	Cooperstown, New York	bone marrow (part of bone involved in blood cell production)
1963	Denver, Colorado	liver
1967	Cape Town, South Africa	heart
1981	Stanford, California	combined heart and lung
1986	Toronto, Ontario, Canada	double lung
1998	Cleveland, Ohio	total larynx (voice box)
1998	Lyon, France	hand
2005	Amiens, France	partial face

This illustration, by sixteenth-century doctor Gaspare Tagliacozzi, shows a method for repairing the lip using skin from the arm.

One of the earliest reports of a successful autograft appears in a work called *Samhita*, which was written in ancient India and which many historians believe to be more than two thousand years old. In it, the writer, Sushruta, describes a method for using skin grafts from the cheek to reconstruct noses and earlobes. Sushruta also described using a forehead flap and other skin grafts to repair disfigured noses. Accounts of similar autografts appear in several medieval texts.

Corneal transplants are the first homografts known to have been successful. The first documented case was reported in 1905 by Dr. Eduard Zirm in Olmutz, Moravia (which is now part of the Czech

Republic). The cornea was from an eleven-year-old boy and the person who received the cornea was an adult laborer blinded by a strong chemical. The man regained the sight in one eye.

The cornea is the transparent layer that covers the front of the eye. Because no blood vessels are involved, corneal transplant surgery today is a fairly simple procedure, usually performed on an outpatient basis. Also, the white blood cells that make up part of the body's immune system, and which would recognize the new cornea as "foreign" material, do not come into contact with the transplanted organ.

Breakthroughs

Early transplant surgeons faced two main challenges: How to join blood vessels and how to prevent organ rejection. Joining a patient's blood vessels to those of the transplanted organ was crucial, because without an efficient blood supply the organ would quickly die. Preventing the patient's body from rejecting (reacting against) the transplanted organ was more difficult. For a long time, doctors did not fully understand how or why rejection occurred, and they were unable to prevent it.

Alexis Carrel, a French surgeon working at the Rockefeller Institute in New York City, pioneered a technique for joining major blood vessels in 1902. Large blood vessels, called arteries and veins, are essentially hollow tubes with walls made up of several layers. Carrel

CUTTING EDGE   MOMENTS

Surgery and embroidery

Alexis Carrel became interested in finding a technique for joining blood vessels after the assassination of the French president by a knife wound in 1894. If surgeons had been able to join the president's severed blood vessels together, the president's life may have been saved. Carrel went to an embroiderer in Lyon, France, to learn to sew with fine needles and thread. He practiced his stitching on paper until he could produce very fine, even stitches that did not go through to the other side of the paper. Only then was he ready to try his sewing technique on actual blood vessels.

dicovered that, if he folded back the ends of each blood vessel like a cuff, he could stitch the inside walls together. This prevented blood from touching any other tissue. He also used a special gel on his needles and threads to help prevent blood clotting. This technique was valuable to many areas of surgery. Carrel was awarded the Nobel Prize for Medicine in 1912. His method paved the way for transplant surgery.

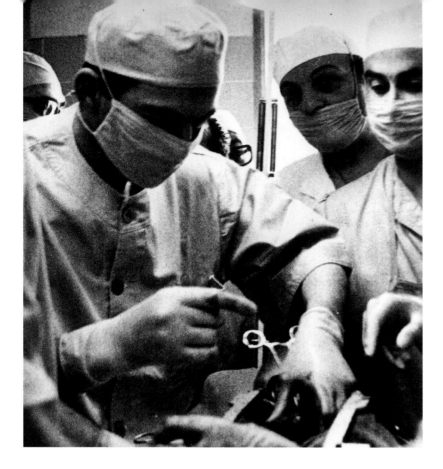

South African surgeon Dr. Christiaan Barnard demonstrates his heart transplant methods on a dog.

Some rejection problem were solved in two main stages. The first breakthrough came in 1909 when Austrian doctor Karl Landsteiner figured out the major human blood groups, or types. His research showed that there were differences between the blood of different individuals. Human blood had four main types, which Landsteiner called A, B, AB, and O. Landsteiner demonstrated that rejection reactions that could cause death occurred when one blood type was mixed with a different blood type. For a transplant to be successful, the patient and the organ donor must share the same blood type. This discovery was an important step toward understanding why some transplants failed. Landsteiner was awarded the Nobel Prize for Medicine in 1930 in recognition of his work.

Advancements in preventing organ rejection did not occur until scientists began to understand the human immune system. The immune system is the body's defense against diseases or "invading" organisms. It also helps the body repair itself. It includes white blood cells, lymph nodes, parts of the bone marrow, and organs such as the thymus and spleen. The immune system detects and removes microbes and anything else that it recognizes as "foreign" and not part of the body.

In 1944, British scientist, Peter Medawar, discovered that animal embryos (animal offspring in the early stages of development) do not reject foreign tissue transplants. At the same time, Australian scientist Frank Macfarlane Burnet showed that the body's immune system learns very early in its development to recognize "self" from "nonself," or foreign tissues. As the immune system develops further, it treats invading organisms as foreign and attacks them.

Medawar and Burnet shared the Nobel Prize for Medicine in 1960. Their research, which studied the early stages of the developing immune system, gave other researchers a much clearer idea of how the organ transplant rejection process worked. Medawar and Burnet determined that, when a patient's white blood cells (WBCs) meet the transplanted tissue, the WBCs recognize proteins on the invading cell surfaces as foreign. The white blood cells then stimulate other blood cells to attack and destroy the foreign tissue.

CUTTING EDGE MOMENTS

The first successful heart transplant

On December 3, 1967, Dr. Christiaan Neethling Barnard performed the world's first human heart transplant at Groote Schuur Hospital, Cape Town, South Africa. The patient, fifty-five-year-old grocer Louis Washkansky, received the heart of someone who died in a traffic accident. Washkansky survived for eighteen days after the surgery, but developed pneumonia and died. Eighteen days may not seem very long now, when patient survival times are counted in years rather than days, but at the time, the event was a truly astonishing achievement.

Improving survival times

Since the first organ transplants were carried out, the advances in the field have led to a considerable improvement in patient survival times. Today, many kidneys still function more than ten years after transplant. More than three-quarters of heart transplant patients survive for at least five years. Doctors and scientists hope that, with further developments in areas such as surgical technique and understanding of the immune system, future transplant patients will enjoy even longer survival periods.

CHAPTER 2

Organ Transplant Possibilities

When people hear about or talk about organ transplants, the organs that first spring to mind are often hearts and kidneys. Many other body organs can be transplanted, however. Organ transplants can be divided into two main groups: tissues, cells, and fluids and complete organs.

Organs that can be transplanted as a whole include those that lie within the chest, such as heart and lungs. Some abdominal organs, including the pancreas, liver, kidney, and small intestine, can also

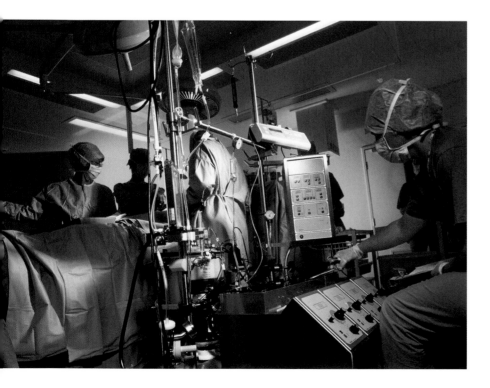

Heart-lung machines, like the one at the front right in this picture, keep a patient's blood circulating and oxygenated while undergoing heart surgery.

be transplanted. In recent years, techniques for transplanting body parts, such as hands and faces, have also been developed.

Heart and lung transplants

The heart carries out the vital process of pumping blood around the body. If the heart stops beating, oxygenated blood can't make it to the brain, and brain death begins within about four minutes. Surgeons need to keep the blood circulating in order to perform many kinds of "open-heart" surgeries. (The term "open-heart" means that a patient's chest is cut open and the surgeon works on the exposed heart.) Surgeons need to keep a patient's blood circulating while performing heart surgery to repair the heart or to replace it with a donor organ without killing the patient.

In 1953, after more than twenty years of research, American surgeon John Gibbon managed to develop a workable "heart-lung machine." Gibbon's machine took over the tasks of pumping a patient's blood (the heart function) and replacing waste carbon dioxide in the blood with oxygen (the lung function) during surgery. Surgeons connected a patient's blood supply to the heart-lung machine and operated on the patient's heart without affecting the blood circulation. This technical development also made heart transplants theoretically possible—thanks to the heart-lung machine, a patient could be kept alive while his or her heart was removed and another put in its place.

CUTTING EDGE MOMENTS

Multiple organ transplants

On March 22, 1997, eight-month-old Eugenia Borgo of Genoa, Italy, received seven abdominal organs. Doctors monitored her very closely, and she recovered well. On January 31, 2004, six-month-old Alessia di Matteo, also of Genoa, Italy, became the first person to receive eight new abdominal organs. She suffered from a digestive system disorder from which she soon would have died. At Jackson Memorial Hospital in Miami, Florida, doctors transplanted a liver, stomach, pancreas, small intestine, large intestine, spleen, and kidneys into Alessia. The donor was a baby boy who had died from a heart disorder. Unfortunately, Alessia never fully recovered and died on January 12, 2005.

The heart-lung machine also made lung transplants possible. Using this machine, circulation of the patient's blood and the exchange of oxygen and carbon dioxide can be maintained while a whole lung or part of a lung is removed. A healthy lung or part of a lung can then be put in its place and the patient's normal circulation resumed. In some patients, heart and lungs are transplanted at the same time. These operations are known as combined heart and lung transplants.

Transplanting abdominal organs

The liver carries out many essential functions within the body, such as breaking down toxins, storing fats, producing blood-clotting factors, and helping to break down old blood cells. If the liver becomes damaged or diseased, however, its function may be impaired, and a liver transplant may be necessary. All or part of a liver may be transplanted.

All the solid organ transplants discussed so far involve removing all or part of a patient's sick organ and putting a new one in its place. Kidney transplants are different, though. The kidneys filter the blood, removing waste chemicals and excess water to form urine, and ensuring the correct balance of salts is maintained. If the only problem is the failure of the kidneys to clean the blood efficiently, the patient's kidneys are left in place. A healthy kidney

CUTTING EDGE   SCIENTISTS

Joseph E. Murray

Joseph E. Murray was born on April 1, 1919, in Milford, Massachusetts, and earned his medical degree at Harvard Medical School in Boston. Murray and his colleagues became intrigued by tissue and organ transplants. Through contact with Sir Peter Medawar (*see page 11*), Murray developed his transplant techniques. On December 23, 1954, he performed the first kidney transplant at Peter Bent Brigham Hospital (what is now Brigham and Women's Hospital) in Boston. Following this achievement, Joseph spent the rest of his medical career in the field of transplant medicine. In recognition of the importance of his work on transplants, Joseph Murray shared the Nobel Prize for Medicine in 1990 with E. Donnall Thomas.

is transplanted into the patient's body, usually above the pelvic bones around where a front trouser pocket would be. However, in cases such as when a patient has cancer of the kidney, the patient's kidneys are removed, too.

Another organ that is sometimes transplanted is the pancreas. The pancreas produces insulin, which is essential for controlling the amount of sugar in the blood. If a person's pancreas does not function properly, there may not be enough insulin to control his or her blood sugar levels. People with this condition are said to be diabetic. One solution to this may be a pancreas transplant. As with kidney transplants, a patient's own organ is left in place when a pancreas transplant is carried out. The new pancreas is transplanted into the lower abdomen.

If a patient who is diabetic also has kidney failure, a pancreas and kidney transplant may be carried out together, with both new organs being put into the lower abdomen. For some diabetics, an alternative to a complete pancreas transplant is a transplant of special groups of pancreatic cells, called "islets of Langerhans," that produce insulin.

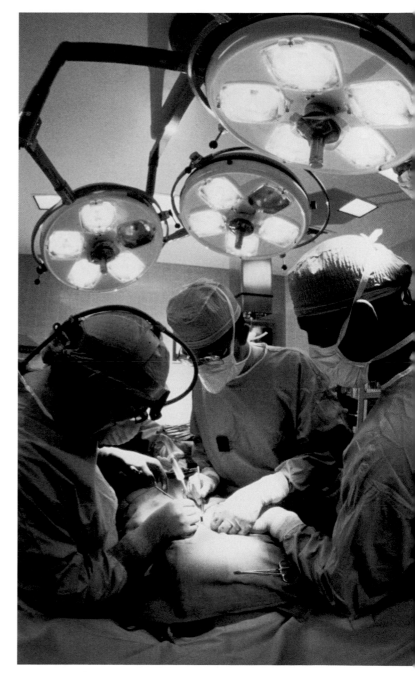

Surgeons carry out a kidney transplant operation.

These are injected into the patient's liver, where they settle and are able to function as they normally would in the pancreas. Scientists are developing ways of coating these cells to "hide" them so that the patient's white blood cells do not detect them and reject them as "foreign."

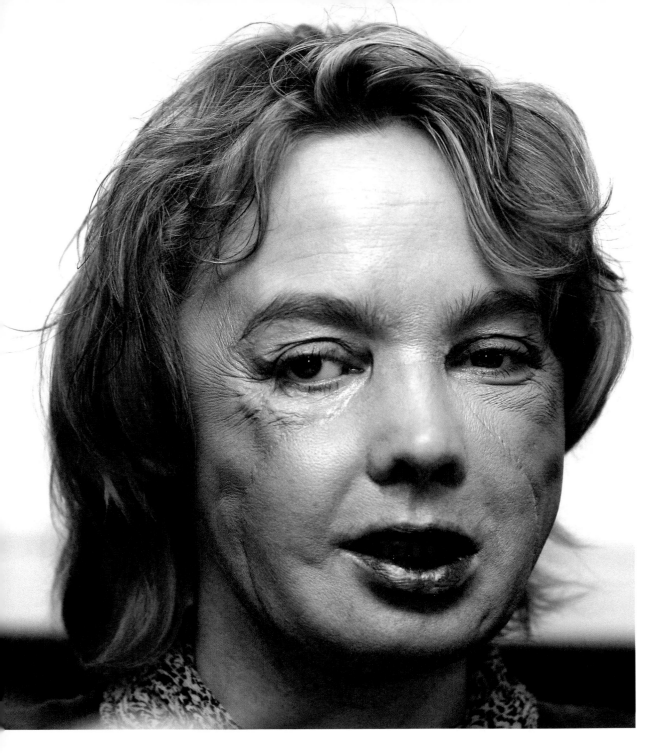

Transplanting body parts

In recent years, surgeons have begun to develop techniques for transplanting various body parts.

Hand In September 1998, in Lyon, France, surgeons Bernard Devauchelle and Jean-Michel Dubernard, in a transplant team led

Isabelle Dinoire, about ten weeks after her pioneering partial face transplant. Scars are visible where old and new facial tissue meet. Her nose, lips, chin, and part of her cheeks are "new."

by Professor Dr. Earl Owen, Director of the Centre for Micro Surgery in Sydney, Australia, performed a hand transplant on Clint Hallam, who was originally from New Zealand. He had cut off his hand with a circular saw while in prison. Although the transplant surgery was successful, Hallam failed to follow the steps for taking the required medications. The transplanted hand was removed in February 2001.

Tongue The first human tongue transplant occurred in Vienna, Austria, in 2003 when a forty-two-year-old man suffering from cancer of the tongue and jaw received a tongue from a deceased donor.

Forearms (and hands) Also in 2003, the first double forearm transplant occurred at the Innsbruck University Clinic, Austria. The recipient, forty-one-year-old Franz Jamnig, had lost both his arms in a work-related accident.

Partial face In 2005, surgeons in Amiens, France, transplanted the nose, lips, chin, and cheek tissue onto a woman whose own face had been seriously injured in an attack by her pet dog.

CUTTING EDGE — FACTS

The first partial face transplant

The first partial face transplant was carried out in Amiens, France, on November 27, 2005. Thirty-eight-year-old Isabelle Dinoire had been attacked by her dog six months earlier, in May 2005. Her nose and mouth were ripped off, and—in addition to destroying her features—the injury left her unable to chew or speak. Surgeons removed the equivalent skin, muscles, and nerve tissue from the face of a female donor. The fifteen-hour operation was successful, leaving Dinoire with a minimum amount of scar tissue.

Dinoire's new face does not look exactly like that of the donor because of differences in the underlying bone structure of the two women. The visible part of the new face does not look exactly like Dinoire's old face, either, again because of differences between the two women's skin and muscles. A key nerve was also missing from the lower part of the donated tissue, which causes numbness and makes normal lip movement difficult.

Thumb Thumb transplants are relatively common. Without a thumb, a person's hand function is severely limited. In cases where a thumb is lost, most often in an accident, surgeons replace the thumb with one of the patient's own great toes (commonly called the "big" toe). Although the transplanted toe is often larger than the thumb it replaces, the great toe functions well as a thumb substitute, and the patient regains fairly normal hand function. Losing the great toe has little effect on the patient's ability to walk—but it may affect his or her balance.

Transplanting tissues

Tissues that can be transplanted include bone, skin, cornea, tendons, ligaments, arteries, veins, and heart valves. More than a quarter of a million tissue transplants occur each year in the United States. Corneal transplants are more common than any other type of transplant. Corneas and heart valves can only be obtained from deceased donors. Many other tissues not vital to life can be autografted or obtained from living donors or cadavers.

Skin can be cryopreserved (preserved by freezing) for up to four weeks for treatment of burn victims. Skin grafts used for other procedures can be frozen for longer periods. For periodontal work (surgery on the tissues that surround the gums and root of teeth), skin can be freeze-dried and stored for up to five years. Skin cells can be grown over a mesh in a laboratory, to increase the area of damage that it can cover.

Skin can also be stretched by inserting a balloon that is slowly inflated over time. The balloon is filled with saline (salt) solution, and more saline is gradually added as the skin stretches. The balloon remains under the skin for several weeks or months, depending on the size of new skin required.

Bone tissue can be transplanted, either as small fragments to stimulate a patient's own bone growth or as larger fragments to replace pieces of damaged bone. Fresh bone tissue must be used within twenty-four hours of harvesting, but it can be cryopreserved

CUTTING EDGE   SCIENCE

Burns and skin grafts

Skin grafts are most often used to treat burns. The outermost layer of skin is made of dead cells that protect the body from moisture loss and infection. Cells from this layer normally wear away throughout the day. Below this is a layer of living cells that divides to produce new cells, replacing those that are lost. Deeper, underlying tissue layers contain blood vessels, nerve endings, sweat glands, and other structures. A minor burn may simply damage the dead outer layer, and cells below divide and repair the damage fairly quickly. In a more severe burn, deeper skin layers are also damaged, and the skin needs help to repair itself. A skin graft of transplanted tissue provides a new foundation on which natural skin cells can anchor themselves for growth.

Donated bone tissue can be ground up, frozen, and stored until needed for a transplant. Bone tissue is often used to replace diseased bone or to fill in spaces around a joint replacement. Donated bone is carefully screened to ensure the health of the recipient.

for up to five years. Tendons, cartilage, and ligaments can also be transplanted to repair damaged joints.

A coronary bypass operation is an excellent example of a common type of autograft surgery. It involves replacing one or more blocked coronary arteries with blood vessels from elsewhere in that patient's body. Coronary blood vessels supply blood to the heart muscle itself. Fatty deposits sometimes accumulate inside the vessels, blocking the heart's blood supply. A complete blockage in one of these arteries can cause a myocardial infarction—the medical term for a heart attack. To treat or prevent this, surgeons remove an artery from elsewhere in the body, such as the thigh, and transplant it onto the heart. The "new" vessel bypasses the blocked vessel and restores an adequate blood supply to the heart muscle.

Transplanting cells and fluids

Although we may not think of blood as a tissue, that is exactly what it is. Like skin tissue, donor blood can be stored and transplanted ("transfused") into another person. Blood components include red blood cells (RBCs), white blood cells (WBCs), platelets, blood plasma, and bone marrow cells. People need blood transfusions for many different reasons, such as to replace blood lost during surgery, an illness, or an accident.

Blood transfusions Blood transfusions of blood components occur every day all around the world. A patient may receive "whole" blood, "packed" RBCs, WBCs, platelets, plasma, clotting factors, or antibodies—depending on his or her need.

Blood cells Healthy people often donate their blood to medical facilities. People with certain illnesses can even donate their own blood before a procedure and have it transfused back into their body as required. Donated blood may be stored whole or broken into its components for future use. Plasma and platelet donors donate only part of their blood, but can do so more frequently than whole-blood donors because they do not donate the oxygen-carrying RBCs.

Government standards control the storage of whole blood and blood components. Whole blood stays fresh for up to twenty-one days after collection. Plasma is usually frozen and used within one year. Platelets must be used within five days of donation.

CUTTING EDGE   SCIENCE

What is blood made of?

Blood tissue has several components. Red blood cells transport oxygen around the body and give blood its red color. Red blood cells are so small that it would take more than one hundred twenty of them to make a line 1 mm long! White blood cells defend the body against germs and disease. Most are larger than red blood cells. Platelets are tiny fragments of cells. They play an important part in helping blood clot after a cut or other injury. The liquid part of blood is called plasma. It is clear and watery and has a pale yellow color. Plasma contains dissolved salts and other chemicals that are transported around the body.

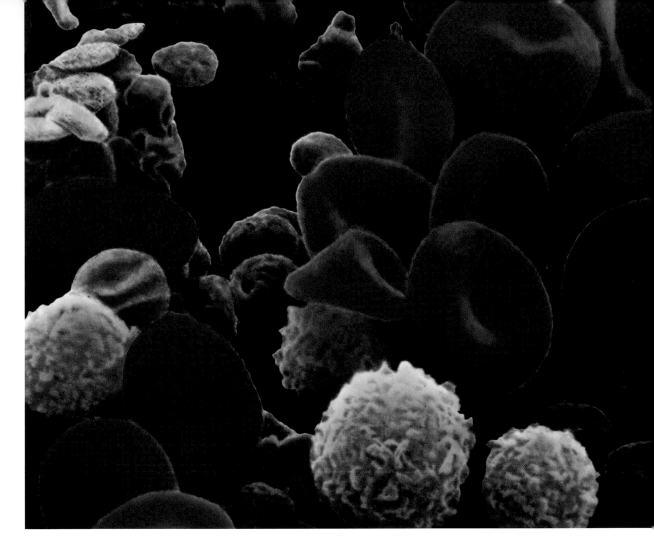

Bone marrow cells Some diseases, such as leukemia, affect the function of the white blood cells. Bone marrow plays an important part in the production of white blood cells, so a disease such as leukemia can sometimes be cured by a bone marrow transplant, which replaces the diseased white blood cells with healthy ones. Donating bone marrow is a more complex procedure than donating blood. In an adult, bone marrow is only actively produced in certain bones—usually those that are wide and flat, such as the hip bones (pelvis), skull, breastbone (sternum), ribs, and thighbones (femurs). The pelvis is the most common site from which bone marrow for donation is removed.

Donors receive a general anesthetic (a drug that causes them to lose consciousness) so they do not feel any pain during the procedure. While the donor is under anesthetic, the surgeon uses a special hollow needle to remove the bone marrow from the donor's pelvis. Donor marrow is transplanted into a patient whose own bone marrow is unable to produce normal blood cells.

An electron micrograph shows human red blood cells (red disks), white blood cells (yellow), and platelets (pink).

21

CHAPTER 3

Sources of Organs

Developing the techniques for successful organ transplants is one thing, but obtaining the organs for transplantation is another. This chapter looks at the three main sources of organs for transplantation. These are:

1. **A living donor.** A living donor can include the patient him- or herself; a close relative of the patient, such as a sister, brother, mother, father, or child; an unrelated donor; or even another transplant patient.
2. **A brain-dead donor or a cadaver donor.**
3. **Other sources.** These can include animals, artificial organs, or newly grown organs.

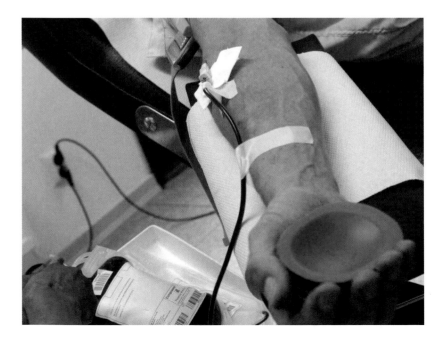

A blood donation involves collecting blood via a needle inserted into an arm vein. The donor occasionally squeezes a rubber object to help increase the blood flow to the arm, decreasing the time it takes to fill the collection bag with blood.

Organs from living donors

Obviously, a living donor can only donate certain tissues or organs. The most common donation a living donor can give is a blood donation. Other living donor tissues or organs include bone marrow, blood components, a lobe of the liver, or a single kidney. Such donations seldom have a negative effect on a donor's health. Even so, doctors must be very sure that the donor understands any risks involved in the donation. For example, undergoing general anesthesia is always a risk, no matter how healthy a person may be. Doctors must also be sure that the donor is donating his or her tissue or organ willingly and is not being forced into it by other people. In some countries, such as Iran and India, people sell tissues or organs for money. Most countries, however, outlaw an exchange of money for organs or tissues—with the exception of whole blood, plasma, or other blood components.

Organs from the patient A patient can donate his or her own tissues and fluids for transplant. Blood can be taken from a patient before an operation, stored, and then used for transfusion during or after the operation. Another example is skin tissue taken from one part of the body and used to repair damaged skin at another part of the

CUTTING EDGE   FACTS

How can you become a donor?

It is not difficult to become an organ donor, but different countries have different regulations. In some countries, donor information is included on drivers' licenses, while in other countries separate donor cards are carried. Regulations for donors in the United States differ from state to state. For example, in California, a donor must be at least eighteen to independently sign a donor card—although with the permission of a parent or guardian, a young person can sign up for the organ registry between the ages of thirteen and seventeen. In England, people can carry a donor card, but unless they have it with them at the time of death, their wishes may not be followed. Registering with England's Organ Donor Register is a more reliable way of ensuring a person's organs will be donated. People under sixteen years can register as long as they have the consent of a parent or guardian. Older people can register as long as their organs are healthy.

body. Because no tissues from another source are used, success rates of such transplants are extremely high.

Organs from related donors For a successful transplant, the donor organ or tissue must match the recipient's tissues as closely as possible. The donor and recipient must have the same blood type. They must also have the same, or very similar, tissue types. Tissue type is determined by the genetic information carried in every cell in the body. This genetic information determines body features and characteristics, such as eye color and nose shape. It also determines characteristics that we cannot see, such as blood and tissue types. In the same way that members of a family often have similar physical characteristics, they also often have similar tissue types. Tissue types of siblings (brothers and sisters) or parents and children are usually the closest matches. Transplants between close relatives, therefore, often have the best chance of success.

Organs from unrelated donors If no suitable related donor is available, an organ from an unrelated donor may be used instead. Rigorous testing is essential to ensure that the donor has a very close tissue type match. Without these tests, the transplant is unlikely to succeed.

CUTTING EDGE   SCIENCE

Using organs from living donors

Many factors must be considered when using an organ from a living donor. Obviously, the organ donor must not be harmed, so the donor's general health and ability to recover from the operation are important considerations. The quality of the organ to be donated is also important, since only healthy organs are suitable for transplant. Medical staff must be very sure that the donor offers the organ of his or her free will and is not being forced into it either by other family members or by his or her sense of duty or responsibility. Medical staff must also be sure that donors understand what they are agreeing to and are fully aware of any possible health consequences. For example, kidney donors should be aware that if their remaining kidney fails, they will require a kidney transplant themselves.

Databases of willing donors help doctors locate specific types of
tissue or organs. When a patient needs a transplant, a database
search can quickly identify a suitable donor. If one database leads
to a dead end, a wider search, often involving several databases in
other states or countries, occurs. If no suitable donor is found
through the database, appeals for volunteer donors may appear in
the media. In some cases, unrelated donors remain anonymous.
Neither patient, nor donor, nor families know anything about each
other. In other cases, patient, donor and families learn information
about each other and may even meet.

**A technician analyzes
samples to check tissue
types and ensure their
suitability for organ
transplants.**

This kidney will be transported to the operating room for immediate transplant into the recipient. Organs for transplant must be kept moist, sterile, and at a suitable temperature during transport.

Organs from other transplant patients How can an organ recipient be an donor at the same time? Picture this scenario: Patient A has a healthy heart but diseased lungs, while patient B has healthy lungs but a diseased heart. The tissue types of patient A and patient B must match. Sometimes, however, a transplant operation is more successful when performed as a combined heart and lung transplant instead of just a lung transplant. Say that patient A's heart and lungs are removed and replaced with the combined heart and lungs from patient C, who has died. Patient A's healthy heart is separated from the diseased lungs and transplanted on its own into patient B. This way, both patient A and patient B benefit from the heart and lungs of deceased patient C. This type of transplant is called a "domino" transplant because the first transplant makes the second transplant possible—just as knocking over one domino makes another one fall, and another, and so on.

Deceased donors or cadavers

Many people who die, either from natural causes or unexpectedly, have healthy organs that could help other people live. For example, a person who dies from head injuries sustained in a traffic accident may have a healthy heart, lungs, liver, pancreas, and kidneys. These could all be used to save the lives of people who are waiting for a transplant of one of these organs.

Many people have already decided which of their organs may be used after their death. They will place a donor sticker on the back of their driver's license or register with an organization that locates donor organs. In other cases, medical staff may ask relatives for consent to remove organs. Making such decisions immediately after the death of a loved one can be extremely difficult, and many organs that could have saved other people's lives are wasted.

CUTTING EDGE   MOMENTS

"Domino" transplants

"Domino" transplants occur infrequently. The very first occurred in 1987 in Baltimore, Maryland. Clinton House's lungs were incurably damaged by cystic fibrosis, an inherited lung disease. Surgeons realized that a combined heart-lung transplant would be more successful than a lung transplant alone. Clinton House received the heart and lungs from a traffic accident victim. Clinton's own healthy heart was transplanted into another man (John Couch), who suffered from untreatable heart failure. In this way, the heart and lungs from a single person saved the lives of two people.

Sometimes, organs are removed from people who are not technically dead, but who are not "alive"—in the usual sense of the word. Modern medical equipment can keep a person "alive" long after that person's brain has died. Doctors must be absolutely certain that there is no brain activity in such a donor before removing any organs for transplant.

Strict guidelines control these situations. In most countries, tests on the potential donor must be conducted at least twenty-four hours apart by two independent doctors—neither of whom is involved in a transplant program.

An electroencephalogram (EEG) monitors electrical activity in the brain. If the EEG shows no electrical activity, the person is considered "brain dead." This person's brain is so badly damaged that it cannot carry out any functions at all, not even basic life processes such as maintaining breathing. The patient has no chance of recovery. At that stage, organs for transplant may be removed. If any electrical activity occurs, the patient may still have some slight chance of recovery and, however limited that recovery may be, the patient's continued existence must take priority over any potential transplants.

Living donors often donate organs and tissues such as bone marrow, blood, skin, a single kidney, and parts of their liver, lung, small intestine, and pancreas. A deceased donor, or cadaver, is a source of vital organs, such as the heart and the complete liver and lungs. For example, the corneas, kidneys, heart, lungs, liver, small intestine, and pancreas from a single donor could benefit as many

CUTTING EDGE   DEBATES

Attitudes to transplants

Many people think that organ transplants are good because they help to save lives. Other people disapprove of transplants for cultural or religious reasons. Some believe that scientists should be allowed to make as much progress as possible in the field of organ transplantation. Others believe that, by carrying out transplants, humans are meddling in things that they should leave to God or some other higher power. Some believe that it is wrong to mix parts of different people together while others think that this does not matter. It is all a matter of opinion. What do you think?

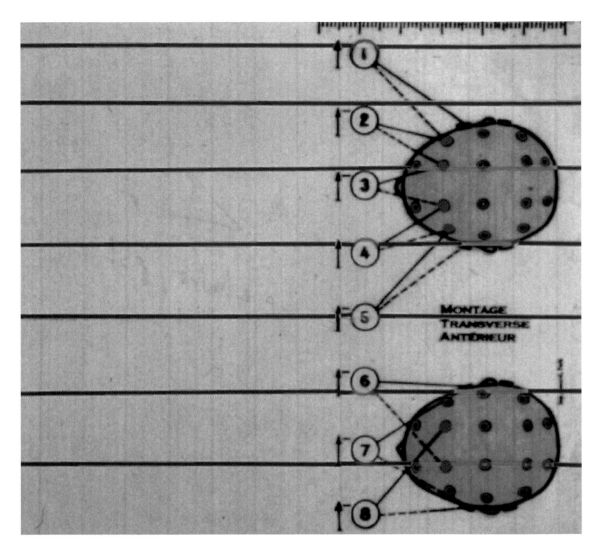

as eleven different people. Even more recipients may benefit if tissues such as bone, skin, and bone marrow are used as well.

Organs from other sources

There are always more people waiting for transplants than there are organs available. Doctors and researchers often seek organs from other sources. Organs and tissues from animals, such as cows and pigs, have been transplanted into humans. Artificial organs, such as mechanical hearts, have been developed. Stem cells—cells that can develop into any type of cell—may in the future be used to grow new organs in the laboratory. Each of these is discussed in more detail in Chapters 5 and 6.

The flat brainwaves (the main horizontal lines) in this EEG show that there are no electrical impulses being produced by this brain, so it is considered dead. To obtain an EEG, electrodes are attached to a person's head. The locations of electrode placement appear as pink dots on the heads.

CHAPTER 4

The Transplantation Process

Every transplant operation requires careful planning and organization. A suitable donor organ must be found and transported to the correct place within very tight time limits. At the same time, the recipient must be assessed and prepared for the operation. The transplant surgery requires a skilled medical team. Afterward, the recipient must be monitored carefully. All of these must occur to ensure that the transplantation process is carried out smoothly and efficiently.

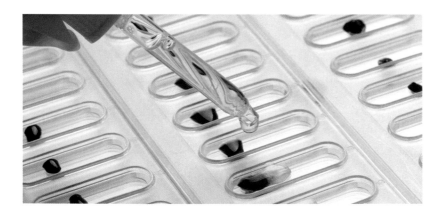

Here, a patient's blood type is being determined. Blood antibodies (agglutinins) are added by pipette. The reaction of the blood drop in each compartment—either no clumping or visible clumping (also called "agglutinating")—indicates the blood type.

The first step in the transplantation process is the assessment of a recipient to determine if he or she could benefit from a transplant. This involves rigorous physical and psychological testing. The patient's condition must be serious enough to require a transplant, yet the patient must be well enough in other ways to recover from the surgery. Doctors also need to be sure that the recipient can mentally cope with the transplant and follow the directions for taking the necessary medications after the operation. The recipient's body also must be hardy enough to withstand the dampening of the immune system caused by the immunosuppressive drugs. He or she must not have a condition that would worsen because of the transplant. For example, the recipient cannot suffer from cancer or from acquired immune deficiency syndrome (AIDS).

Once a recipient has been identified as needing and being suitable for a transplant, the search for a suitable donor organ begins. National and international registries keep current information about available donors and organs. The recipient's blood type is determined by separating blood cells and mixing them with specific antibodies (chemicals produced by the immune system to recognize and attack the foreign protein on cell membranes). Each antibody attacks a specific antigen (the foreign protein that stimulates antibody production). If an antigen is present on the blood cells, the antibody sticks to it. Laboratory instruments detect when an antibody and antigen stick together. By combining the results, technologists can determine which antigens are present in the blood sample. From that information, they determine the tissue type, which is vital when matching a recipient to a donor organ. A recipient may wait a long time for an organ, but once a match is confirmed, preparations for the transplant procedure can begin.

CUTTING EDGE SCIENCE

Waiting for transplants

The length of time a person must wait for a transplant depends on several factors, including:

- blood and tissue type—potential recipients with rare blood and tissue types often wait longer for a match than those with more common blood and tissue types;
- the type of organ needed—some organs (such as kidneys and corneas) are more readily available than others;
- medical urgency—if only a single organ is available, the recipient with the greatest medical need will receive it while others wait;
- time already spent on waiting list—a potential recipient who has already waited a long time for a donor organ may receive one before a recipient who was just added to the list;
- distance—the closer the donor organ and the recipient, the better the chance for a successful transplant.

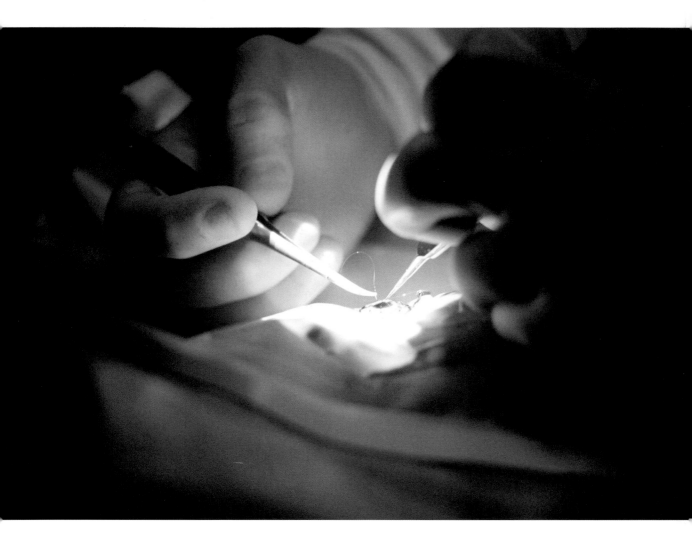

As soon as the patient has been notified that an organ is available, he or she needs to get to the hospital quickly. At the same time, the organ will begin its journey to the hospital. Before the transplant can proceed, the patient's health must be assessed again. The transplant may be cancelled if the patient has an infection or if another problem arises.

A surgeon stitches a donor cornea onto a recipient's eye.

Corneal transplants

A corneal transplant is performed if a patient's cornea (the clear layer covering the front of the eye) is damaged through injury or illness. The donor cornea can only be removed from a deceased donor. The corneal transplant operation, which is also known as keratoplasty, is usually carried out with a local anesthetic. The patient is awake throughout the surgery but feels no pain because the eye is numbed. The doctor performs the operation using a surgical microscope, an instrument that gives the surgeon a magnified view of the eye as he or she operates. The eye is measured, and the donor cornea is cut to the right size and shape. An instrument called a trephine cuts out the damaged part of the recipient's cornea. The donor cornea is then positioned carefully and stitched into place. After the operation, a soft eye patch covered by a hard shield protect the eye and help prevent injury. Eye drops minimize risk of infection. The stitches may be removed after a few months or may be left in place permanently. Vision usually returns slowly, with most patients regaining good eyesight within one year. The cornea has virtually no blood supply, so rejection of the transplant is unlikely.

Bone marrow transplants

Some forms of anemia, leukemia, Hodgkin's Disease, and other white blood cell cancers and tumors damage bone marrow. Normal production of white blood cells is prevented, and the immune system cannot function properly. Bone marrow transplants can restore white blood cell production and immune function.

Before a bone marrow transplant occurs, the recipient usually receives very high doses of radiation therapy (radiation treatments) and chemotherapy (drug treatment). These are aggressive treatments that destroy the recipient's immune system so that it cannot attack the transplanted cells. It also kills any quickly dividing or diseased cells, such as cancer cells. The bone marrow cells are then transplanted directly into the recipient's bloodstream by "infusion"—a tube inserted into a vein, called an intravenous (IV) tube.

Once in the bloodstream, the transplanted cells should migrate to the recipient's bone marrow, where they grow and produce new blood cells. The white blood cell count of the recipient's blood is monitored for several weeks until doctors are sure the transplant has worked and new blood cells are being produced. During this time, the patient must be protected from infection.

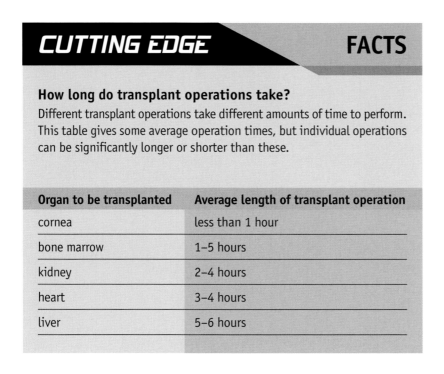

CUTTING EDGE — FACTS

How long do transplant operations take?
Different transplant operations take different amounts of time to perform. This table gives some average operation times, but individual operations can be significantly longer or shorter than these.

Organ to be transplanted	Average length of transplant operation
cornea	less than 1 hour
bone marrow	1–5 hours
kidney	2–4 hours
heart	3–4 hours
liver	5–6 hours

Kidney and pancreas transplants

Kidneys filter waste chemicals and excess water from the blood. If the kidneys do not work properly, the blood does not get "cleaned," and a person can become extremely ill. Several conditions cause kidney failure, including diabetes, hypertension (very high blood pressure), and glomerulonephritis (chronic kidney inflammation).

A kidney transplant is performed while the recipient is under general anesthesia. If the donor is living as well, he or she is given a general anesthetic. Microsurgical methods (surgery carried out through several small incisions, using magnified views and special instruments) often minimize the stress of the operation on the donor. A small part of each of the donor kidney's main blood vessels—the renal artery and renal vein—are left attached to the kidney. A small length of the ureter, the tube that carries urine from the kidney to the bladder, must also be left attached to the kidney. An incision is then made in the recipient's abdomen, above the pelvic bones, and the kidney is sutured into place, somewhere near the natural kidney, which is usually not removed. The renal artery and vein of the donor organ are stitched to the major blood vessels that carry blood to and from the recipient's leg. The donor ureter is stitched to the recipient's bladder, and the abdomen is closed. The amount of fluid drunk and urine produced by the recipient is monitored closely to ensure the transplanted kidney begins to function normally.

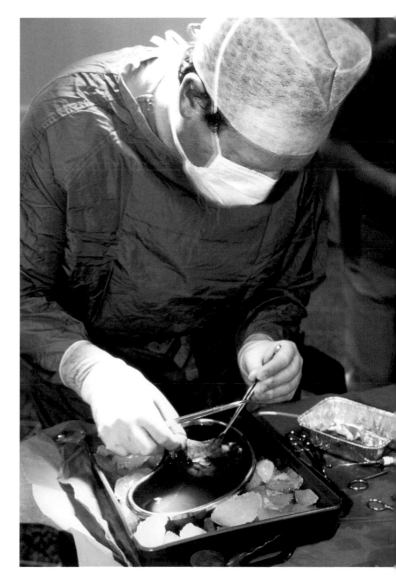

The kidney shown here is being prepared for transplant. The surgeon is removing fat from around the kidney. A special solution is flushed through the attached blood vessels of the organ before transplantation.

A pancreas transplant is carried out in a similar way to a kidney transplant. The recipient's own pancreas is not removed, and the new pancreas is transplanted into the lower abdomen. Again, the blood vessels of the pancreas are attached to the blood vessels of the recipient's leg. As well as secreting insulin into the blood, the pancreas also secretes other substances via a duct (tube) into part of the small intestine. Therefore, a small piece of donor small intestine, with the duct draining into it, is removed at the same time. The donor intestine is surgically attached to the recipient's bladder or intestine to drain the secretions from the donor pancreas after the operation.

Some patients who are diabetic (*see page 15*) also suffer kidney failure, and a pancreas transplant alone would not solve their problems. In such cases, a kidney and pancreas can be transplanted at the same time. As with the single organ transplants, the recipient's own kidneys and pancreas are left in place, with the new organs transplanted into the lower abdomen.

Heart transplants

A heart transplant may be necessary in a patient whose heart has become weakened by disease or illness. A major cause of heart failure is coronary artery disease (often caused by genetic factors, smoking, lack of exercise, obesity, viruses, and other causes). Another major cause of heart transplants is cardiomyopathy, an inefficient, weak heart the cause of which is often unknown.

Patients waiting for a heart transplant are usually extremely ill and close to death. Symptoms of acute heart failure include weakness, pallor, and shortness of breath. Many patients are confined to a wheelchair or bed and can only take a few steps at a time. They often need an oxygen supply to help them breathe. For patients in this condition, a heart transplant is not just a lifesaving operation—it also allows them to lead an active life and do things they may not have been well enough to do for years.

A heart transplant is carried out while the recipient is under general anesthetic. The surgeon opens the chest through an incision in the patient's sternum. His or her blood supply is connected to a heart-lung machine that will take over the function of the heart and

CUTTING EDGE SCIENTISTS

Sir Magdi Yacoub

Heart transplant surgeon Magdi Yacoub was born in a village in Egypt on November 16, 1935. His father was a general surgeon, and when Yacoub was a young boy, he knew that he wanted to be a surgeon, too. Yacoub was educated in Cairo, Egypt, and earned his medical degree there in 1957. In 1962, he moved to London, England, where he became a consultant cardiac (heart) surgeon. Yacoub specialized in working with children with congenital heart defects (defects they were born with). He conducted complex operations on very young babies. In England, Yacoub was also involved with the first heart transplant and performed the first "live" lung lobe transplant (using lung tissue from a living donor).

Magdi Yacoub retired in 2001, but still conducts research on stem cells, organ rejection, and xenotransplants and is involved in the development of artificial heart valves. He received many awards for his outstanding work and was knighted in 1992. Yacoub established the international Chain of Hope charity to provide free heart treatment to sick children from poor and war-torn countries.

Egyptian-born cardiologist Sir Magdi Yacoub is famous for his pioneering work in heart transplant surgery.

lungs during the operation to keep the recipient alive. The diseased heart is removed, and the new heart is put into the chest cavity and stitched into place. Blood vessels are reconnected, and the recipient's blood is allowed to flow through the heart.

In most cases, as blood flows through the transplanted heart, it begins beating. If it does not start beating again, surgeons may use an electric shock to restart the heart. Once a regular heartbeat is established, the recipient is disconnected from the heart-lung machine. The chest cavity is closed with stitches or clips. The recipient will spend some time in intensive care, but should be able to get up within a few days.

Lung transplants

The lungs oxygenate the blood and remove carbon dioxide waste. If the lungs are damaged so that this cannot occur, a lung transplant may be necessary.

For a lung tranpslant, the recipient is under a general anesthetic, and a large incision is made in the chest. For a single lung transplant, this may be either through the sternum or horizontally from below the shoulder blade around the side to the front. The surgeon collapses the diseased lung and severs the blood vessels and airway. The sick lung is removed, the new lung put in its place, and the airway and blood vessels are reconnected. Throughout the operation, the remaining lung continues to function normally. For a double lung transplant, the incision is under the ribcage, from one armpit to the other. The single lung transplant process is then carried out twice over. At some point during this operation, the recipient will probably be connected to a heart-lung machine.

Once the lung or lungs have been stitched into place, the chest incision is closed and stitched or clipped. The air that remains in

In this liver transplant operation, the donated liver is ready to be stitched into place in the recipient's abdomen. The ice helps keep the liver fresh.

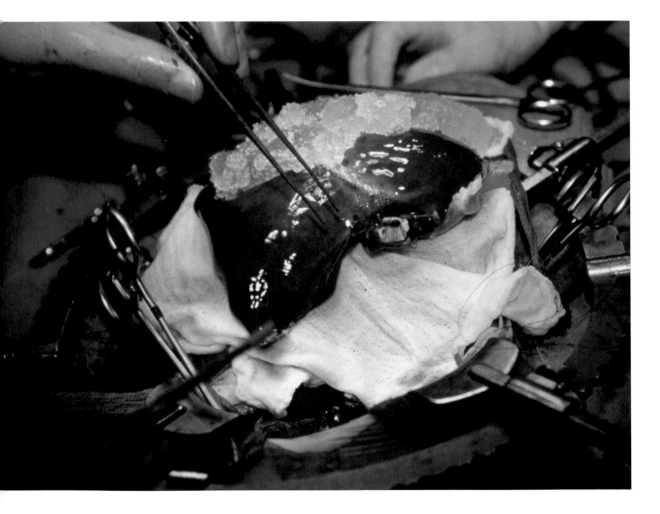

CUTTING EDGE   SCIENCE

Variations on basic transplants

In some cases, variations on a basic heart, lung, or liver transplant are required. Some examples appear below.

● In some cases, both the heart and lungs are damaged. These patients may receive a combined heart and lung transplant using similar techniques to those described on these pages.

● Two patients can benefit from a single liver if a split liver transplant can also be performed. For this procedure, a liver is split into two sections and divided between two recipients. This technique is possible because a person can be healthy with less than a whole liver. The liver's structure does not allow splitting it exactly in half, so the recipient with the greater need receives the larger portion (60 percent) and the other recipient receives the smaller (40 percent) portion.

the chest cavity from the operation is removed via a drain to allow the transplanted lung to reinflate. This drain is removed when the chest wound heals. After the operation, the recipient will need to spend several days in intensive care and may need the assistance of a mechanical ventilator to assist in normal lung function until the recipient's transplanted lungs are fully functioning again.

Liver transplants

Liver failure may make a liver transplant necessary. Two major causes of liver failure are alcohol abuse and infection by the disease hepatitis C. Another cause of liver failure is primary biliary cirrhosis, a condition in which liver tissue is slowly destroyed.

With the recipient under a general anesthetic, the surgeon makes a large, curved incision in the upper part of the abdomen. The sick liver is removed, and the new liver is put in its place. Blood vessels and bile ducts are reattached. A small tube may be put in to drain fluid away from the bile duct. This fluid collects in a small bag outside the body. Other tubes may also be inserted to drain fluid from around the liver. The liver is stitched into place, and the abdominal incision is closed and stitched. The recipient spends some time in the intensive care unit. When the recipient has recovered and is ready to leave the hospital, the drains are removed.

Skin transplants

If skin is so badly damaged that it cannot repair itself, a skin transplant may be needed. Skin transplants are often necessary in cases of severe burns, large wounds, some surgical procedures, and some cosmetic surgery.

Depending on the extent of the skin damage, a skin transplant may be carried out under local or general anesthetic. If the recipient is undergoing an autograft, a skin-cutting instrument called a dermatome will remove skin from another part of the body, such as the buttock or inner thigh.

The graft tissue is spread over the damaged area and held in place by a padded dressing or stitches. The area from where the

A surgeon prepares donated bone for a bone transplant operation. The surgeon reshapes the bone before implanting it.

CUTTING EDGE   FACTS

How do patients feel after a transplant?
How a patient feels after a transplant differs depending on the type of organ that has been transplanted. For example, a patient who receives a corneal transplant will feel very different from one who receives a heart transplant. Once the initial surgical recovery period is over, most transplant patients feel much better than they did before the transplant. Their quality of life is much improved, and they are able to do many things that their ill health previously prevented. Most transplant recipients are extremely grateful to the donor who made the operation possible. Occasionally, a recipient is unable to accept the fact that his or her body contains an organ from someone else; that organ recipient may require psychological counseling.

graft is taken must also be covered with a dressing to prevent infection. For a larger area of damage, a flap of skin, together with underlying muscle and blood supply, may be transplanted. The skin transplant is monitored for several weeks to ensure that blood circulation is established. Recipients are often advised to avoid stretching the transplanted area during this time.

Bone tissue transplants

Bone tissue transplants are carried out for several reasons, including reconstruction of damaged or deformed bones and bone repair after treatment for bone cancer.

A bone tissue transplant can replace or repair damaged bone. The operation is usually carried out under a general anesthetic. The surgeon makes an incision in the skin above the bone. Donor bone tissue is shaped to fit and then inserted into the space where it is needed. Many times, screws, pins, or plates hold the transplanted bone in place. The incision is then closed and stitched.

To prevent the transplanted bone tissue from moving while it is healing, a splint or plaster cast is often applied. The length of the recovery period varies, depending on how much bone tissue was transplanted and the site of the transplant.

A recipient is often advised to limit the amount of exercise he or she undertakes for several months after the transplant in order to allow the bone to heal fully.

After the operation

Doctors monitor an organ recipient's health for a long time after a transplant operation. While the recipient is still recovering in the hospital, his or her condition will be monitored continuously. Some medical tests are specific to a particular type of transplant. For example, most lung transplant patients undergo lung function tests, such as exercising while being monitored with an instrument called a spirometer. The lung condition is checked by bronchoscopy, chest X-ray, and a computer tomography (CT) scan. Heart function tests for a heart transplant patient includes an electrocardiogram (EKG) and echocardiogram (ECHO), and the condition of the transplanted heart may be checked by chest X-ray and CT scan.

Other general tests performed after most types of transplant include the following:

- blood tests—the levels of a variety of chemicals in the blood provide information about how well the transplanted organ and other organs are functioning.
- blood count—the number of red blood cells, white blood cells, and platelets provides information about the health of the organ recipient.
- biopsy—examining a tiny sample of the transplanted organ allows medical staff to check for early signs of rejection.

The number and frequency of tests will gradually be reduced as the recipient's recovery progresses, but he or she may still need to

CUTTING EDGE   SCIENCE

How do immunosuppressive drugs work?

Different immunosuppressive drugs work in different ways, but they all affect the white blood cells to stop them from attacking the transplant. Some block the production and development of new white blood cells. Some, such as cortisone, prevent white blood cells from causing inflammation of the tissue of the organ that is being rejected. Others, such as cyclosporine, prevent white blood cells from producing interleukin-2, a hormone that is needed for the immune system to mount an effective immune response.

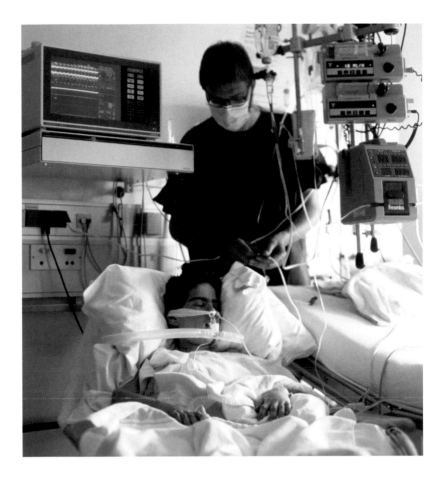

This patient is recovering in a cardiac intensive care unit (ICU). The monitor shows information such as his heart rate and breathing rate.

return to the doctor's office or the hospital for checkups several times a week for several months. If all goes well, the recipient stays healthy, and the transplant is not rejected, the times between checkups will gradually increase. Many transplant recipients have a yearly exam for the rest of their lives.

Immunosuppression

The main danger after a transplant is rejection, even when tissue types have been carefully matched. The recipient's body may still reject the transplanted organ at virtually any time. To prevent this, the recipient must take a combination of drugs to stop his or her immune system from working. This is called immunosuppression. These drugs do not prevent the immune system from attacking just the transplant—they stop it from attacking any "foreign" cells or organisms. The recipient is therefore unable to resist infections and may need strong antibiotics to stay healthy.

CHAPTER 5

Overcoming Problems with Organ Transplants

Organ transplantation may seem like a miracle treatment for some illnesses and conditions that would otherwise be fatal. Although organ transplants can save lives, the different types of surgeries also raise some problems.

Organ shortage

Donor organ shortage is a big problem for most transplant programs. National and international transplant registries store information about possible donors and transplant recipients. These transplant registries must act rapidly to match donors with recipients to ensure that no organ is wasted. International cooperation allows worldwide donor and recipient matches.

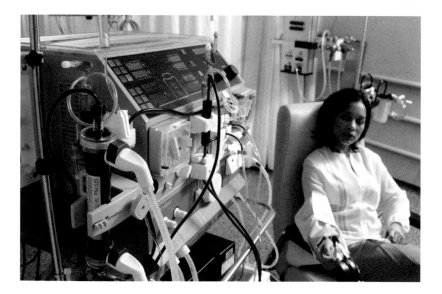

Many patients with kidney failure depend on dialysis machines like this one. The process of filtering the blood takes several hours.

Another way of tackling the shortage problem is to find substitutes for a failing organ. At present, no organ substitute is ideal for long-term use, and most are used as a "bridge to transplant"—a way to simply keep a patient alive while he or she waits for an available organ. Progress in the development of artificial organs is more successful for some organs than others.

Artificial organs

Dialysis machines have been generally available since the 1960s as a mechanical substitute for the blood-filtering function of the kidneys. A tube carries blood from the patient's arm into the dialysis machine, which removes waste chemicals and ensures the correct levels of minerals, salts, sugar, and water are maintained. The blood then flows back into the patient's arm via a second tube. For many patients, dialysis means lengthy hospital visits several times a week. Such visits can disrupt a child's education and make it impossible for an adult to hold a job.

Smaller dialysis devices have been developed for patients to use in their own homes, but these take up considerable space. The machines are also costly, and not available for every patient who would benefit from them.

A more recent innovation consists of a portable device coupled with an osmotic membrane (a thin layer that allows some substances to pass through it) that is implanted in the abdomen. The device must be connected to a small external machine, usually on a daily basis, to complete the dialysis process.

None of these methods of dialysis, however, provides an ideal long-term solution. The majority of patients with kidney failure hope to someday have the chance for a kidney transplant that will allow them to live a more normal life.

CUTTING EDGE   FACTS

Finding more donors

In some countries, people who wish to become donors must register with the appropriate organization. These organizations must check detailed information about each donor. Vital time can be lost between a potential donor's death and the release of his or her organs for transplant. Some governments are considering turning the system the other way around so that everyone would be considered a willing donor unless he or she had registered a refusal. Although this would increase the number of donor organs available for transplant, some people oppose the idea, and the matter is still under discussion. Advertising and education also help make more people aware of the donor organ shortage, in the hope that it will persuade them to register as organ donors.

The development of an artificial heart has long been a goal for many scientists. Paul Winchell patented the first artificial heart in 1963. His design formed the starting point for Robert Jarvik, who was affliated with the University of Utah Medical Center in Salt Lake City. Jarvik developed an artificial heart called the Jarvik-7. Its first use occurred at the University of Utah Medical Center when it was implanted into sixty-one-year-old retired dentist, Barney Clark on December 2, 1982. Clark survived for 112 days after the operation.

This experience encouraged researchers to continue improving the Jarvik-7. It and other subsequent models, however, required external power supplies in the form of large battery packs. The battery packs were heavy and about the size of a refrigerator, restricting the patient's mobility.

A Jarvik-7 artificial heart is implanted into a patient's chest.

On July 2, 2001, a fifty-nine-year-old retired librarian, Robert Tools, received the first AbioCor Implantable Replacement Heart at a hospital in Louisville, Kentucky. Tools's new heart had few moving parts and was made of special plastic and titanium—which made it safe for contact with blood. The revolutionary design of the AbioCor included both an external and internal batteries that could power it for up to half an hour. This allowed recipients to disconnect themselves from the external battery pack for short periods—for example, while they took a shower or bath.

The introduction of the Berlin Heart marked another milestone in the development of an artificial heart. The Berlin Heart sits outside the body to function as a ventricular assist device (VAD). It helps either of the ventricles (the heart's lower chambers) of the heart pump blood. If both ventricles are failing, two Berlin Hearts can be used, one for each ventricle. The pump, which is driven by compressed air, is connected to the heart and blood vessels by tubes. Although the Berlin Heart has been used in isolated cases in the United States, they are not approved for general use there. Other types of VAD can be used, though. Some can fit inside the chest, virtually "piggybacking" onto the patient's own heart.

CUTTING EDGE MOMENTS

Artificial hearts for babies and children

Some babies are born with defective hearts, and others develop heart problems during childhood. Many of these babies and children can be treated by surgery. In some cases, however, a heart transplant is the only option. If a child becomes dangerously ill while waiting for a donor heart, the child may receive an artificial heart to get through the waiting period. This has only become possible in recent years because the small size of a baby's or young child's body makes it difficult to develop a suitable artificial device. An extra-corporeal membrane oxygenator (ECMO) machine can take over the function of the heart and lungs for up to twenty-one days. After that time, complications, such as blood clots, internal bleeding, or kidney problems, often develop. The development of the Berlin Heart, which can be made as small as a golf ball, means that even very young babies can be helped. Since the first Berlin Heart was used in 1990, the device has saved the lives of many children as they wait for a suitable donor heart.

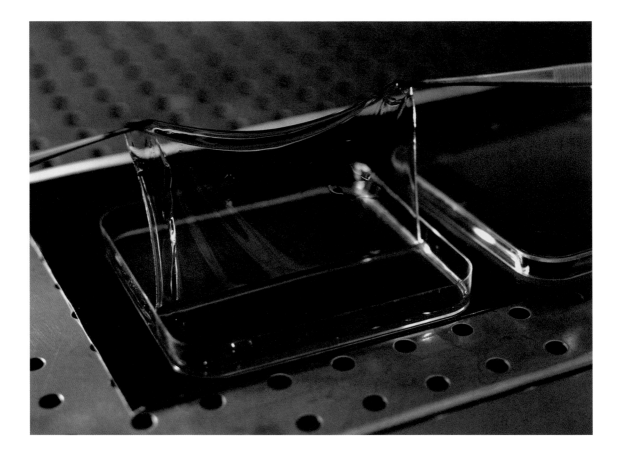

Patients waiting for a liver transplant may receive an artificial liver. This device combines a pump and cloned (grown from a single cell in the laboratory) human liver cells. As blood is pumped through the device, the liver cells carry out normal liver functions, such as filtering out toxins (poisons) and producing proteins.

Patients waiting for a lung transplant can use implantable synthetic lungs (intravenous membrane oxygenators, or IMOs) temporarily. An IMO consists of a bundle of hollow fibers with a balloon at the center. It is injected into a leg vein and guided through the blood vessels to the vena cava—the large blood vessel that carries blood to the heart. Once in position, the balloon inflates and deflates about one hundred times a minute, drawing blood through the fibers. Oxygen enters the blood and waste carbon dioxide is removed.

Artificial skin has been developed and transplanted successfully by a number of research teams, including one at the University of Illinois in Chicago. One method combines natural collagen, a

Artificially grown skin is removed from a culture dish for use in a skin transplant operation. It takes about three weeks to grow 1.2 square yards (1 square meter) of skin. Artificial skin can be used to help burn victims whose injuries are so severe that little healthy skin is left on their own body from which to grow a skin graft.

fibrous material, and a synthetic polymer mesh (human-made netting). Microsponges of collagen form in the spaces of the polymer mesh. This provides a framework on which skin cells can grow. The resulting substance, when used to cover an area of damaged skin, supports the growth and development of new skin. An alternative substance is a self-repairing artificial skin. This contains microcapsules that are filled with a healing chemical. If the artificial skin cracks, the microcapsules break open and the chemical is released into the crack, helping to repair it.

Growing new organs

Another approach to overcoming the shortage of donor organs is to develop a method for growing new ones. Some teams of researchers are investigating ways of using stem cells for this purpose. By taking growing stem cells in the laboratory, researchers hope to use stem cells from a patient's body to grow new tissues and organs for transplant, which will decrease problems with rejection.

Some researchers have discovered that it is possible to use other body cells for growing new organs. In April 2006, researchers in the United States reported that they had successfully grown new bladders from patients' own bladder cells in the lab and then transplanted the bladder cells back into the patients. The advantage of using a patient's own cells is that the organs are the same blood and tissue type as the patient's, so there is no risk of rejection.

Rejection of transplants

A second major problem with organ transplants is the rejection of a transplant by the patient's immune system. There are two main

CUTTING EDGE   SCIENCE

What are stem cells?
At the earliest stage of an embryo's development, its cells have the potential to differentiate into any type of cell. These undifferentiated cells are called stem cells. They can form lung, muscle, bone, nerve, or any other kind of body tissue. Once the stem cell's genetic information instructs it to develop in a particular way, however, it matures into a specific type of cell. It cannot then change into any other type of cell.

ways of combating rejection. One way is to ensure that the donor organ and recipient are as similar as possible. Accurate tissue typing, which enables close matching of the donor organ and recipient, lessens the likelihood of the recipient's immune system recognizing the organ as foreign and aggresively attacking it. The other way of avoiding rejection is to suppress (restrain) the patient's immune system. To do this, radiation therapy (treatment involving radiation), immunosuppressive drugs, or a combination of both, are used. If the immune system is suppressed, it cannot attack the donor organ, and rejection does not occur.

Early attempts at immunosuppression used radiation therapy alone. During the 1960s, a limited number of immunosuppressive drugs became available. For more than twenty years, transplant patients endured treatments that combined drugs and radiation therapy. In the 1970s, a more sophisticated approach incorporated drugs that targeted specific cells in the immune system. As scientists expand their understanding of the immune system, they may develop other medications or treatments that result in fewer side effects for transplant patients.

CUTTING EDGE   SCIENCE

What are the risks with immunosuppression?

Although immunosuppression helps prevent rejection, it also causes some problems. One function of the body's immune system helps provide protection against germs. Suppressing a patient's immune system makes a patient more vulnerable to infections. An infection, such as a common cold, that poses little risk to a relatively healthy person can quickly become a life threatening problem for someone with a suppressed immune system.

Another function of the immune system is to detect and destroy abnormal cells, such as cancer cells. A suppressed immune system cannot do this, so immunosuppression can lead to an increased risk of cancer. Radiation therapy and immunosuppressive drugs themselves also have unpleasant side effects, such as hair loss, vomiting, diarrhea, kidney and liver damage, and digestive system problems. Radiation therapy is especially detrimental because it targets not only cancer cells but all swiftly dividing cells in the body, including hair follicles and the intestinal lining. The destruction of these cells causes hair loss, vomiting, and diarrhea.

In some cases, particularly with bone marrow transplants, a graft-versus-host (GVH) reaction occurs: The immune system cells of the transplanted organ react to and attack the recipient's cells. Strong doses of powerful drugs help treat a GVH reaction.

Surgical techniques

Performing an organ transplant requires skilled surgical techniques. Considerable progress in this field has occurred since the earliest transplant operations were performed. Consequently, most transplant procedures carry less risk than before.

Bone marrow transplants carry the risk that the transplant will reject the recipient. To help avoid this possibility, the donor bone marrow is treated with antibodies that purge it of the white blood cells that might launch an attack.

Progress in surgical techniques has benefited living donors as well as transplant recipients. For example, until the mid-1990s, people who donated a kidney underwent a major operation. This involved a large—about 10-inch (25-centimeter)—incision, that cut through abdominal muscle. Donors also had to agree to the loss of a rib so that surgeons could access their kidney.

Today, surgeons use keyhole (laparoscopic) surgery, in which a small incision—about 3 inches (7–8 cm) wide—is made near the navel. Four other small holes are also made in the abdomen for insertion of surgical instruments.

The donor is left with a much smaller scar and recovers more quickly than from traditional surgery. In addition to the benefit to the donor, laparoscopic surgery has also increased the number of live kidney donors, since more people are willing to undergo this less-invasive procedure.

Surgical advances that evolved from developments in medical technology and equipment are often used during transplant operations. For example, magnetic resonance imaging (MRI) and computed tomography (CT) scans—techniques for viewing the inside the body—provide valuable health data as well.

Also, advances in computer technology make it possible for surgeons to view detailed images on monitors during surgery. Tiny

CUTTING EDGE SCIENCE

Robot surgeons?

Robotic technology has advanced rapidly in recent years and some of these advances are of great value to surgeons. It is now possible for a surgeon to operate while sitting beside the patient and looking at a computer screen. The screen shows a detailed image of the area of the patient's body that is to undergo surgery. Special grips connected to the computer control the surgical instruments that are placed inside the patient's body. While watching the image, the surgeon moves the grips, which make the robot move the instruments inside the patient. This amazing technology allows the surgeon to make very accurate movements. It also reduces patient pain during recovery—a much smaller incision is required, since the surgeon does not need to fit his or her hands inside the patient's body. Recovery time is also faster than with conventional surgery.

cameras can be positioned to allow the surgeon to see organs, blood vessels, and other structures from angles that would otherwise be impossible. Surgeons wear special lenses, worn like a pair of eyeglasses, that create a very clear, magnified view for performing intricate surgery.

The surgeon here will never touch his patient. Instead, he controls robotic surgical instruments that perform the operation.

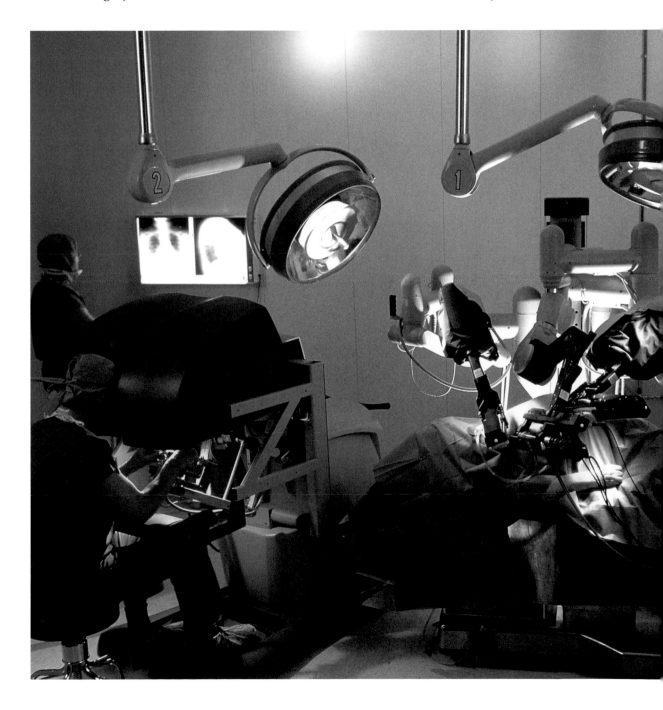

CHAPTER 6

Current Research

Over the last fifty years, scientists and doctors working in the organ transplant field have made tremendous progress. Problems remain to be solved, however, and the search for better technologies, more thorough knowledge, and improved surgical methods continues.

Stem cells

Many scientists think that stem cell research will provide significant advances in organ transplants. Stem cells have the potential to

---

CUTTING EDGE — DEBATES

Ethical issues

There are many ethical issues surrounding the field of organ transplants. Doctors, researchers, politicians, religious leaders, and many other people are involved in discussions about what should and should not be allowed. Different countries have different laws. Some allow procedures that are banned elsewhere. The issues being debated include the following:

Is it right to:

- use animals as a source of organs, tissues, cells, or fluids for humans?
- use human embryos as a source of stem cells?
- alter the genetic information in cells?
- create transgenic animals (*see page 57*)?

What do you think? Is any procedure that can save a human life justified, or should we limit what scientists are allowed to do? If there should be limits, who should decide on and set those limits? Should these decisions be reviewed as science progresses through the years?

mature and develop into every type of body cell. Teams of researchers are experimenting with growing new tissues and organs from stem cells. If a patient's own stem cells could be removed and stimulated to develop into a new organ, the new organ could replace a failing or diseased organ. Two of the main transplant problems would be solved: The patient's immune system would not reject its own tissue, eliminating the need for immunosuppression therapy and, organs would be readily available for transplant.

Artificial organs

Researchers seek to improve existing artificial organs and develop new types of artificial organs. Early artificial organs were designed to copy the exact functioning of the organ they were replacing. Now, many scientists believe that human organs are too complex for this "mechanical copying" to succeed. Instead, researchers are investigating how to grow and manipulate human cells as a means

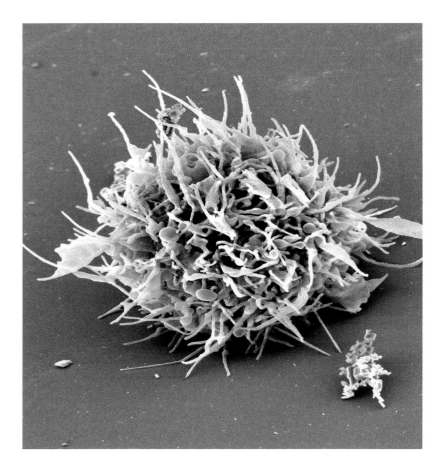

An electron micrograph of a human stem cell. This stem cell has the potential to develop into either a red or white blood cell.

of creating organs. Attempts are also being made to develop organ-like devices that combine artificial parts with living cells. An example of this is the artificial liver (*see page 48*).

The combining of artificial and living cells is considered a hydbid technique: two different components function as one unit. If the hybrid techniques prove successful for other organs, this research will provide devices that can be used instead of human organs and help provide a solution to the problem of donor organ shortages.

CUTTING EDGE   FACTS

Hiding transplanted cells

Scientists searching for ways to combat rejection have developed materials that can be used as a barrier between transplanted cells and the recipient's body. For example, using a semipermeable polymer membrane developed at Charles University, Prague, in the Czech Republic, scientists have been able to implant cells into the brains of patients suffering from Parkinson's disease. The polymer acts as a sheath, separating the transplanted cells from the patient's cells. Once transplanted, the cells produce dopamine, a chemical necessary for normal brain function. The dopamine diffuses out through the sheath into the brain. This treatment has helped some patients improve. Doctors are hoping that a similar technique may be used to treat other illnesses, such as Alzheimer's disease and diabetes. Research into the development of an ideal material for the sheath is continuing in many countries, including the United States.

Xenotransplantation

Xenotransplantation is the transplantation of organs betwen animals of different species, including humans. Organ transplants from animals that are closely related to humans, such as baboons and chimpanzees, have not been successful, however. The animal that offers the most promising successes for xenotransplantation into humans is the pig. Porcine organs are similar in size to human organs. Porcine organs are also plentiful because hogs produce large litters, the animals are easy to care for, and they grow quickly. Since 1975, hundreds of thousands of pig heart valves have been used to replace defective heart valves in humans. Bovine (cow) heart valves have also been used since 1981.

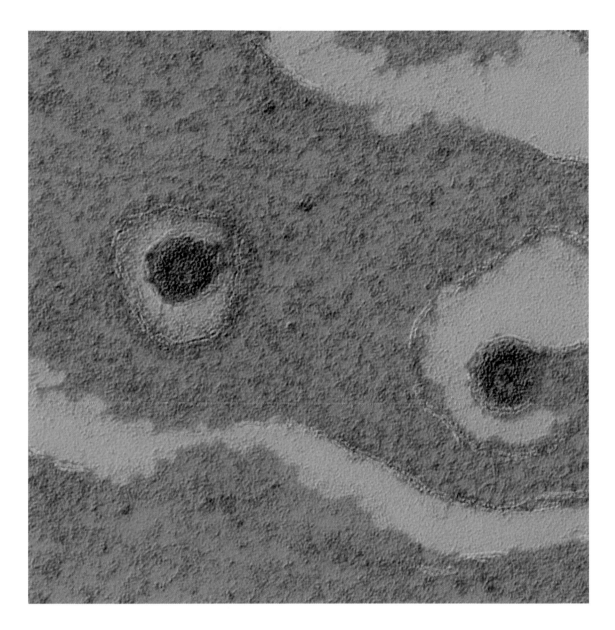

Genetic engineering techniques that delete specific pig genes and replace them with human genes may help reduce the chances of rejection. Mixing the genes in this way would create a "transgenic" animal, which would have both pig and human genes. Much debate concerns whether or not xenotransplantation should be attempted at all. There is a risk that animal viruses may be transferred to humans. Also, the introduction of animal genes into the human gene pool may have long-term consequences that we cannot even imagine at the moment.

This electron micrograph shows the pig virus porcine endogenous retrovirus (reddish) in the process of infecting a culture of human kidney cells (green). This virus does not harm pigs, but the discovery that it can infect human cells has led to concern that it might cause disease if pig organs are transplanted into humans.

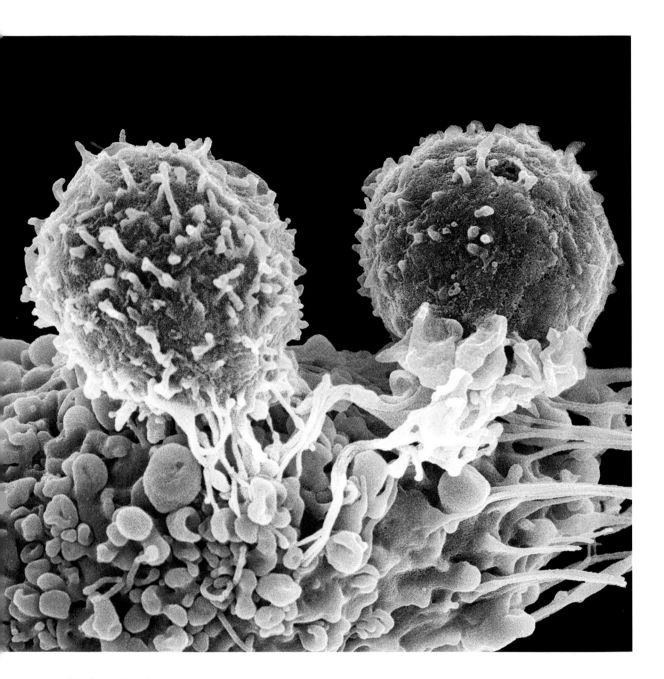

Induced tolerance

During the 1950s, researcher Ray Billingham, working in Oxford, England, conducted investigations that paralleled the work of Peter Medawar and Frank Macfarlane Burnet (*see page 11*). Billingham proved that the immature immune system does not recognize the difference between "self" and "foreign" immediately after birth. In an experiment on newborn mice, he transplanted skin from a black

This electron micrograph shows white blood cells (orange) attacking a "foreign" cell (greenish-blue). Magnification: 4,000x mouse onto the back of a white mouse. Older mice would have rejected the skin transplant, but the newborn mice showed no signs of rejection. Billingham theorized that the immune system might learn to accept, or tolerate, the foreign tissue.

Recently, other scientists have revisited this idea. They have successfully transplanted organs in newborns, even when the tissue types of the donor organ and recipient did not match. The donor organs or tissues came from other babies that died. Some fetuses with life-threatening conditions were put on a transplant list and received a transplant within a few hours of being born. The immature immune system does not recognize the transplant as foreign, and so the babies tolerated their new organ or tissues.

In older children and adults, an infusion of bone marrow cells from the donor before a transplant reduces the risk of rejection. Called "induced tolerance," this technique has been used successfully in some heart and kidney transplants. Research into other methods of induced tolerance continues. If perfected, it would help eliminate donor organ rejection problems for the recipient.

CUTTING EDGE SCIENCE

The Human Genome Project

The genome of a species is the genetic code carried on the chromosomes in the nucleus (the cell's control center) of nearly every cell of an individual. After thirteen years of research, scientists from many different countries worked together and completed the human genome mapping in 2003. Scientists used this information to develop some genetic tests that allow the early detection of rejection by a simple blood test. Scientists also hope to be able to alter specific parts of the genetic code, enabling the body to repair damage or prevent damage from occurring—thus making organ transplants unnecessary. By understanding more about the human genome, scientists will be better able to assess the implications of introducing animal genes into the human gene pool.

There are, in all likelihood, many other ways in which our understanding of the human genome may be used to allow progress in the field of organ transplantation. These could include more accurate matching of donors and recipients; genetic engineering of animal cells to create organs that will not be rejected; and a greater understanding of the immune system and how it can be controlled.

Glossary

abdomen The area of the body between the pelvis and the chest that contains the liver, stomach, intestines, and other organs.

agglutinate To cause cells, such as red blood cells, to stick together in clumps.

antibody A chemical produced by the immune system in response to an antigen.

antigen A substance that the immune system recognizes as "foreign."

artery Any blood vessel that carries blood away from the heart.

autograft A transplant using a person's own tissue, cells, or fluid (also known as an isograft).

biopsy Removal of a small piece of tissue for examination.

bone marrow The innermost bone tissue, where production of white blood cells occurs.

bronchoscopy Examination of the main airways using a tiny camera.

cartilage A springy, fibrous tissue that cushions joints.

cell The tiniest complete unit of a living organism.

chemotherapy Chemical treatment of disease.

chromosome One of the chemical chains that forms during cell division; it carries genetic information.

cornea The transparent layer at the front of the eye.

cryopreserve Preserve by freezing at a very low temperature.

CT scan (Computerized tomography) A type of X-ray that provides detailed, three-dimensional computer images of organs.

dialysis Filtering blood to remove waste chemicals.

donor A person who donates an organ, tissue, cells, or fluid for a transplant.

echocardiogram (ECHO) A test of heart function using ultrasound echoes.

electrocardiogram (EKG) A test that measures the electrical activity of the heart.

gene A small part of a chromosome that carries the instructions for a particular feature or trait.

genetic code The sequence of information carried by the full set of chromosomes.

genetic engineering Altering the genetic information of a cell.

genome The complete genetic code of an organism.

graft Another word for transplant.

graft-versus-host reaction An attack on a transplant patient's tissues by the immune system cells in a donor organ.

harvesting Removing an organ, fluid, or tissue for transplant, testing, or research.

heart The muscular organ that pumps blood around the body.

heart valve One of the two sets of flaps inside the heart that open and close to regulate blood flow.

heterograft A transplant between individuals of different species (also known as a xenograft).

homograft A transplant between individuals of same species (also known as an allograft).

hormone A chemical "messenger" that travels through the blood to affect cells around the body.

immune system The body's defense system.

immunosuppress To prevent the immune system from working.

induced tolerance The prevention of rejection of an organ whose tissue type is different from the recipient's.

kidney An organ that filters blood to remove waste chemicals and produce urine.

ligament A strong band of fibers that holds bones and cartilage in place.

liver An organ that carries out many important metabolic functions, such as removal of toxins from blood.

lobe A rounded division of an organ, such as the lungs or liver.

lungs Spongy organs that allow oxygen to enter the blood and carbon dioxide to leave the blood.

microsurgery Surgery using magnifying techniques and tiny instruments.

nucleus The part of a cell that contains the chromosomes and controls cell functions.

organ A group of tissues that work together.

pancreas The organ that regulates the level of sugar in the blood.

plasma The clear, straw-colored liquid part of blood.

platelets Tiny cell fragments that help blood to clot.

radiation therapy Medical treatment that uses repeated doses of radiation, such as X-rays and gamma rays, to control cancer.

rejection An attack by a transplant receipient's immune system on the donor organ.

saline Containing salt.

semipermeable membrane A thin, flexible sheet that allows only certain types or sizes of molecules in a solution to pass through.

spirometer An instrument that measures lung function and efficiency.

stem cell A cell that has the potential to develop into any other cell type.

syngeneic graft A transplant between genetically identical people (identical twins).

system A group of organs that work together to perform a specific function.

tendon A strong band of tissue that attaches a muscle to a bone or a muscle to another muscle.

tissue A group of similar cells that make up a body part.

toxins Poisons produced by organisms, especially bacteria, which are capable of causing disease.

vein Any blood vessel that carries blood to the heart.

ventricle A lower chamber of the heart.

X-ray An image of the body obtained by using a beam of radioactive waves.

Further Information

BOOKS

Ballard, Carol. *The Immune System.* Body Focus (series). Heinemann Library (2003).

Bankston, John. *Christiaan Barnard and the Story of the First Successful Heart Transplant.* Unlocking the Secrets of Science (series). Mitchell Lane Publishers (2002).

Fullick, Ann. *Organ Transplantation.* Science at the Edge (series). Heinemann Library (2002).

Kerrod, Robin. *Medicine: Present Knowledge—Future Trends.* 21st Century Science (series). Smart Apple Media (2004).

Parker, Steve. *Heart, Blood, and Lungs.* Understanding the Human Body (series). Gareth Stevens Publishing (2005).

Townsend, John. *Scalpels, Stitches and Scars: A History of Surgery.* A Painful History of Medicine (series). Raintree (2006).

WEB SITES

www.ustransplant.org
Check out the official organ transplant registry Web site for the United States.

www.donors1.org
Read about one of the oldest and largest organ and tissue procurement organizations in the United States.

www.marrow.org
Visit the National Marrow Donor Program Web site and register to save a life.

www.classkids.org/library/classqa/bloodtyp.htm
Discover more information about how blood types affect organ donations.

www.biology.arizona.edu/Human_Bio/problem_sets/blood_types/inherited.html
Find out about how blood types are determined.

Publisher's note to educators and parents:
Our editors have carefully reviewed these Web sites to ensure that they are suitable for children. Many Web sites change frequently, however, and we cannot guarantee that a site's future contents will continue to meet our high standards of quality and educational value. Be advised that children should be closely supervised whenever they access the Internet.

Index

Index *(continued)*